My Life, My Prayer

360-Degree Life Turn Around Recipe

Gloria and Larry Ovie

Michael Terence Publishing

First published in paperback by
Michael Terence Publishing in 2019
http://mtp.agency

ISBN 9781913289522

Gloria and Larry Ovie have asserted their right to be identified as
the authors of this work in accordance with the
Copyright, Designs and Patents Act 1988

Copyright © 2019 Gloria and Larry Ovie

All rights reserved. No part of this publication may be reproduced,
stored in a retrieval system, or transmitted, in any form or by any
means, electronic, mechanical, photocopying, recording or
otherwise, without the prior permission of the publishers

Cover image
Copyright © Akz & Irochka

Cover design
Copyright © 2019 Michael Terence Publishing

Contents

Introduction 1
Foreword 5

1: Identifying Your Real You 9
2: The Skill Factor 15
3: The Brand Foundation 21
4: It's Time for Total Clean-Up 27
5: Seed Gathering 37
6: Understanding True Success 43
7: Becoming a Disciple with Distinction 49
8: Do Not Rest on Yesterday's Victory 57
9: From Instruction to A Turnaround 63
10: Breaking the Wings of Fault Finders 69
11: Dangers of Unnecessary Worries 75
12: Surviving in a Two World Order 81
13: It All Begins With Questioning 87
14: One Key to a Turn Around, Prayer 93

PRAYER POINTS:
Marital Blessing 101
Breaking Barriers 103
Declare Promotion 105
Your Business Success 107

Freedom from Death 109
Power Against Evil Dreams 111
Overcoming Forces of Darkness Called Wasters . 113
Total Deliverance 115
Divine Favour 117
Place an Embargo Against Unwanted Happening
.... 119
Show Yourself Oh God 121
Removing Evil Marks 123
Promise and Fail 125
Divine Healing 127
Academic Success 129
Shake Them Away 131
Deliverance from Temptation 133
Pursue and Recover 135

Prayer 137

Contact Gloria and Larry Ovie 138

Other Books by Larry Ovie 139

Introduction

This book is a guided revelation that will open you up for a guaranteed 360-degree life turn around. Revelation brings realization, and realization brings liberation. Revealed knowledge is the antidote for deception.

The greatest obstacle to success is deception, and this book has unveiled many secrets that are been used by the world enemies to hinder many from success.

Prayer is the desire, opportunity, and privilege of talking with God. For your prayer to be effective, you must understand the importance of your relationship with whom you are praying to and why you should pray.

God gave us the earth as a gift to subdue, maintain and keep for our pleasure, but note this: Without man, God will not do anything on earth.

From creation God gave the man all the powers over the earth, for this reason, there must be a partnership between heaven and earth because the creator has the code to the created.

God is supreme and never goes against his word. He made us as spirits living in bodily forms on the face of the earth.

God is spirit and for him to accomplish anything on earth, He needs a body to do that. It will be a violation of man's sovereignty if He comes in a spirit form to the earth.

Prayers create intimacy between you and God, who is always waiting for you to call on Him, not only at the time of need but for a continued fellowship.

To be able to stand the wiles of Satan on earth you must call on God who has the power to silence the devil.

It does not matter what you believe or what your faith is, you will always pray to something higher than you.

The enemy cannot afflict you without legal ground, so if he does not find one, he creates one to attack you.

In this book, there are revelations that will help you avoid the traps of the wicked, and guarantees a 360-degree life turn around.

This book is written by the inspiration of God with revelation and our personal family testimonies.

Prayer must be your way of life if you really want to succeed.

Starting your day with prayers is taking ownership of

your life.

Ownership brings responsibility, responsibility brings drive and drive brings achievement.

Man, essentially is a Spirit, he has a soul and lives in a body. The spirit of man is created in God's likeness and can relate directly to God.

The soul of man gives him a distinct personality. And with his body, man can relate to the physical world.

Every man is created to fulfill a purpose.

Your purpose on earth is your reason of been created and each man's success is marked by such achievement.

After a clear understanding of our state on the face of the earth, we must know the weapons we need for this warfare. Of everything you will do to succeed in life, the most important is prayer.

Foreword

I am honoured to have been asked by Pastor Larry Ovie to write the forward for this book which I can identify with so easily because it addresses some topics I have taught students in my MIB (Motivate * Inspire * Build) class, and deals with issues many of my mentees would have raised when in sessions with me. This is a powerful book by Pastors Larry and Gloria Ovie and is so apt for this time.

In the intro to the book, the line "The greatest obstacle to success is deception" speaks volumes, and gives an insight into the secrets of hindrances, that will be unveiled to you as you read. Many struggle with, and in life, and feel stuck, finding it hard to move forward. This is the book you need to help you get unstuck.

Its breaks down Prayer, the tool through which we communicate with God, and expands on the importance of understanding the essence of a relationship with whom you pray to and why you should pray. Many Christian perish for lack of knowledge. This is another opportunity to get knowledge and understanding.

One of the big challenges in the world today is that many do not actually know who they are. A major reason is because they are reading from someone else's script, trying to act out a role. As a consequence, many have become untrained accidental actors, faking it and hoping to make it someday.

This book challenges you to take the bold step to begin to truly know yourself and be yourself without the need to act or make-believe. It gives relatable insights into how you can identify the real you, in order to be able to know your true self.

In reality, many do not know themselves and as a result, are caged under the shadow of someone else's personality. It's time to break away from under that shadow and this book will help you do just that, in a simple and practical way.

It is not just enough to know yourself. Once you do, what do you then do with what you know? In this book, you will learn how to identify your skills (which are your gifts), how to develop them on time through training, and how to use them to focus on your goals in life.

You will also learn about building or rebuilding on a solid personal foundation, the power that lies in being able to build your own personal brand without abusing it, the significance of surrounding yourself with the people who can help you become better and the power of knowing and applying the word of God in your life.

This book is loaded, and as you begin to read, I want to encourage you to focus (this is a word I love and something I have perfected the act of doing over years that has helped me this far), as distractions abound. The examples are very simple to relate to everyday life and will help you give a deeper meaning to the topics.

If you truly want to understand and learn real success, if you want to stop borrowing and move on from past to new victories, then make the choice now to unlearn and read this book with an open mind, so you can re-learn new ways to save/invest, look far ahead, stop worrying unnecessarily, and summon the courage to call the bluff of fault finders in your life.

As a bonus, you will find therein powerful prayer points with scriptures that come in handy for many life situations that require God's intervention.

You were created for a purpose, and if you still struggle with discovering your purpose or you want clarity on what your purpose is, this is the book for you.

Like I always charge everyone who encounters me, I want to charge you now; that once you have read this book and you are blessed, do not keep it to yourself, pass it on by blessing someone else with a copy of this book. Become a strong link in the unbreakable chain of continuous blessings from God.

God bless you and make you a blessing as you read. And as you find your true self and build your way to success, I look forward to seeing you at the top.

Councillor Yemi Adenuga
Navan Municipal District,
Meath County Council
1st African Female Councillor in Ireland
Life & Business Strategist

…She builds people.

1: Identifying Your Real You

The first journey to success is knowing who you are. When you look at the mirror what do you see? A quote from Be Gretchen.

"My first commandment is to "Be Gretchen"—yet it's very hard to know myself. I get so distracted by the way I wish I were, or the way I assume I am, that I lose sight of what's actually true."

The only person in the dream of your life is you, and for you to succeed you must first be you.

Pause and ponder for a minute about when you dream, there are always people, known by you and others you might not have a clue about. When you wake up from your dream none of these persons has any knowledge of what transpired in the dream except you.

How well you know yourself and able to accept it will create for you a paradise on earth, many have continually lived under the shadow of others making life unbearable for themselves.

For a 360-degree life turn around, your assignment is first to know who you are, what really works for you as a person. Am I an introvert or extrovert? in what form do

I best function.

How are you energized? do you function better alone or you get more effective with others around you.

Some pointers to knowing who you are…

Get real about yourself
Many are always in the habit of lying to themselves. If you lie to yourself, your real you cease to exist. When you try to be someone else, everything about you changes and it is detrimental to your success.

Your inner peace
This is my biggest pointer to knowing who you are. Do you have inner peace when you act, take a step, in relationship, career? when you look at the mirror are you motivated or waiting for others' approvals or confirmation?

Your peace of mind is so important to your performance in life and your success depends on your performance.

Embrace your imperfections

Everyone has one imperfection or the other. By embracing it you are accepting your real you. It is at this point that you find a place to mend and your unique you come alive.

Your real you is a masterpiece created with a distinct DNA that no one else has, in a nutshell, there is no copy of you anywhere.

This gives you a unique opportunity to be a success, and to be celebrated.

I funnily say something to my congregation's that I am the most perfect being on the face of the earth. If you are taller than me you are too tall, if you are shorter than me then you are too short, if you are slimmer than me then you are too slim and if you are fatter than me then you are too fat.

This is because of the uniqueness of my DNA. I can see an inner smile that says yes this is who I am.

The law of demand and supply says that market forces tend to drop the price if the quantity supplied exceeds quantity demanded, and prices rise if quantity demanded exceeds quantity supplied.

In this case, your nature and uniqueness make you a high flyer as you are the only one who is in demand here.

This is my testimony. Before I got married to my wife, I will literally be everywhere trying to do everything. And she brought it to my notice, that by continuing in this form not only will it lead me astray but it will get to a point where I will not have the energy to continue.

We do not have the whole time in the world to continue life with trial and error.

I took it in and began to narrow down the me that needed to be successful.

At this stage I want you to narrow down whatever you think is your calling, or purpose as it may be, and build your energy around it.

Know yourself, know thyself, and be yourself.

But what exactly does that mean? Is it some cliché, Instagram post or Facebook status? I'll tell you what it isn't, to find yourself, isn't a consequence of any outside forces, actions, beings, or persons. There is nothing outside of whom you are that is the key or gatekeeper to whatever lies within.

The ancient Greeks travelled to the Oracle at Delphi to seek wisdom and knowledge. Before they entered the Oracle, there above the entrance, was in scripted "Gnothi Seauton" or translated "Know Thyself". This saying was purposefully placed above the oracle, and would soon after be a prominent hashtag, as those who seek wisdom must first know who they are before obtaining any wisdom and enlightenment from outside forces.

If you know yourself, you will come to realize that everything that you need is within you. All of the power in the world lies within each and every one of us. It is deep within, waiting to be unburied.

"We say act yourselves, not acknowledging some have never met themselves".

Those who truly know who they are didn't always have the easiest path or journey to self-actualization. They fought with society and the image that they were told to be, and, to play the part. They had battles with their emotions, some they won and many they lost. They went to war with their insecurities, a victory often hard-won.

We don't meet or get to know ourselves just by being born. Birth is something that is gifted, a gift that is unknown to us, at least until we have enough self-awareness to realize the blessing of what it means to be alive. However, being alive and its accomplice of what is called life, is still incomplete if you never find your reason why. Of why you are who you are, of why you were gifted life and to know what it means to be you.

Your real you is the only one that can be celebrated, by knowing who you are, you have set the tone for the victory waiting to happen.

Becoming real about yourself is a key tool for your everlasting peace. Many still struggle on how to put behind their false front that they tend to carry about, a deceptive outward appearance that will only halt you and stop you from any positive move of life.

When you are real about yourself, the greatest killer of dreams will disappear from you, FEAR.

2: The Skill Factor

Skills are the knowledge and ability that enables you to do something well.

After knowing who you really are, you must have identified what you are good at. In life, people exchange money for their skill.

At this junction, I want you to write in a separate sheet several things that you are good at doing.

Most things that you are good at are the naturally inborn gifts that can be transformed into skills.

For you to truly succeed, you need to understand how the skill works, either inborn or acquired, every skill must be developed for it to become a product.

Inborn skill is the natural gift of individuals, could be in music, sport, art, etc, while acquired skill is what you trained to become.

In all this, one thing is prevalent whether it is acquired or is natural it requires development before it could become a product.

Identify to develop

When you identify your gift then it is time to develop it through training.

Let me come in here with a little testimony that could help you take this decision faster.

If you are privileged to have read one of my books titled the power of a circle, you must have read how I struggled to go to school at an early age for lack of sponsorship and the inability to pay my school fees by my parent.

This setback did not stop me to continue to aspire to be educated, this helped me to face the world with courage.

With all the gifts I have in the ministry, I remember in my early years in ministry those who did everything to stop the progress of my ministerial work by putting up campaigns on how I am not educated just to stop me from speaking in a conference, I helped put together today.

Today by determination and encouragement from my wife who is a co-writer of this book, I have since acquired a Bachelor of Arts in Business, Enterprise and Community Development and Bachelor of Arts (HONOURS) in Social Enterprise, Leadership and Management.

The story of George Weah, the Liberian 112th

president.

Many believed his lack of formal education was the reason for his earlier electoral defeats, but Weah was determined not to let this undermine his chances in the 2011 election.

"These are ever-since pictures," the 43-year-old Weah said in an interview with The Associated Press in the eastern Paynesville suburb of Monrovia. "I am now in my senior year and by God's help, I am graduating from college next July".

See:

www.foxsports.com/soccer/story/george-weah-gets-educated-in-quest-for-election-78377895-081110

With his determination to lead his people, he knew that training and going back to study is the only way he can increase the value of his product which is him.

You are the product of your life and the more equip you are the more value you will attract.

I brought these testimonies to encourage you as you think within your inner mind, can I, at this age? I have passed the time and many more that are going through your mind right now.

Note that if you did not take the required steps to train, you will always be in the position to want to be like others and always wanting to sell others product because your product might not be marketable or will not attract the right value.

Get to develop your skill on time in life as it will help you to focus on your ultimate goals in life.

The singleness of your eyes so important, narrow down what you want to do in life and focus with a single eye.

Why do photographers cover one of their eyes before taking a picture? So, they can see a good view of the quality of the picture been taken.

The quality of your life will be determined by the quality of your skill.

What so ever you decide to do in life, train to be the best at it, this will make you indispensable.

Train and retrain

Most of the time we need to upskill as the training you have yesterday might not be relevant for tomorrow's challenge.

I remember as a young boy, I had an in-law who is a

secretary at a mat making company in Lagos, Nigeria.

'In the early stage of this company, all they needed for an accounting position was a typist with good typewriting skills, as there were no computers then.

At the emergence of computers, many of the staff were encouraged to retrain on how to use computers but my in-law refused, as it was looking so new and complicated for him.

Your guess will be the same as mine, he was among the first to be laid off.

Note he was good at what he was doing but for lack of upskilling, he lost his job.

In all, you have to train and retrain at all times to meet the current demands of your market.

This quickly bring us to our personal story the testimony of going back to college. This you can relate with as this chapter will not be complete without getting into the picture of our lives.

Graduation -
Bachelor of Arts (HONOURS) in Social Enterprise,
Leadership and Management

The testimony is not just about the certificate but the added knowledge that it has given to us when dealing with people and our world.

3: The Brand Foundation

Every man is a brand, and the price tag will be determined by how qualitative the brand is. We live in a world where everyone is aspiring, jostling to outsmart each other. It does not matter what side you are, there are those who have made themselves the authority and are not interested that you get to them at the top.

Many do not realize how important to remain clean as they navigate their ways to the top in life, one act of criminality can ruin every chance in making it to the top.

Because there are many obstacles that you need to overcome to rise to the top in the first place, you have to guide your brand diligently.

I want to quickly bring you to the attention of what can happen to your brand if you abuse your brand.

Don't Abuse That Blessing!

There was a certain man in a certain place in Africa.

He was married with five kids.

This man was very poor to a point he could not

afford the school fees of his kids. The good side of him was that he knew God, worshipped God, love his wife and show respect to people. At different occasions his uncle told him to deny God, else he will not assist him financially anymore and in response he told his uncle "My God shall supply all my needs, I do not need your money anymore". Though he was poor he was an icon of emulation to some persons in his community based on his services to God and how humble he is to everyone.

He never gets involved with anything that is ungodly, always upright and this earned him a good brand.

He and his family fasted three times a week. He kept his morning devotion with his family.

He was fondly called the man of Jesus by friends and his acquaintances.

Meanwhile, he was a first-degree holder from one of the reputable universities in the country. One fateful day, God decided to remember him as he did to Mordecai in the Bible. An oil company invited him for an interview on Thursday morning at about 10.00am and the interview went successfully. A week later he was given a letter of employment. The letter stated his monthly salary, allowances, and other incentives. As a matter of fact, the content of the letter was beyond his imagination hence he screamed and shouted on top of his voice eh…! On hearing this, his wife came out asking what the problem was. God has answered our prayers he said.

He went to church and testified and also promised to buy a house for the church. On resumption to work and he was assigned with a car and a chauffeur. A month later the company gave him a duplex to move into his own apartment.

Consequently, a man that was called after Jesus became hostile to God and became so proud.

He abandoned the church who prayed for his employment, telling the pastor that he is now very busy. As if that was not enough, he went into drinking and smoking.

God gave him the blessing so he could be a blessing to humanity but his action proved hostility to God and his family.

He even went further to practice polygamy and having concubines all around, from one city to another.

In view of this, his attention shifted from his wife and children who prayed and also suffered with him.

Where were these women when he was a nobody? Where were these attitudes of his, when there was no money in his pocket? Most people pretend to be good when there is no money, but as soon as they are blessed, they become hostile.

The easiest way to destroy your brand is to be proud. As pride goes before any fall.

Anything that can divert you from the right part of life will destroy your brand which is you.

There is no quick success anywhere, many drug addicts today, were good and normal people with a great life ahead of them before. Out of greed for quick success, many became drug dealers and users thereby destroying their brand permanently.

As these words are echoed into your heart you might just be thinking of one or two celebrities that have fallen from grace to grass because of abuse of drug, substance and many more. Be wise.

In some African nations, for instance, there are political and religious instabilities, some parts are crying for resource control, other parts are crying out against marginalization while some other parts are clamoring for religious rights.

Is it a crime that Africa is blessed? There is a need for Africa to understand the purpose of the blessing.

The brand Africa is suffering because of insecurity and greed. Today many do not want to do business with Africa, making Africa remain a third world country.

Your Beauty is a Blessing from God.

Most women are wonderfully and carefully created by God.

The beauty of a woman is a blessing from God. But it is unfortunate that most beautiful women do not stay with one man, they move from one man to another thereby commercializing their beauties, is beauty becoming a curse? Statistically, the average woman stays with the husband till death do them part.

These short stories are few that I want you to bear in mind when building your brand which is you.

Do not allow anything to stain your brand.

We see many talented people sign contracts with organizations and then get themselves entangled with drugs and other ways of life that put them on the negative side of the law.

What happened to them? There will come an immediate revocation of such contracts as no one want to get involved with such brand that can destroy their brands.

Your brand is you and you must guide it with everything within your power, as it must be protected for it to succeed.

4: It's Time for Total Clean-Up

The effectiveness of every product is determined by what it contains, and when what it contains lose its effectiveness, the only option will be to flush it out or clean-up in order to prepare for the next phase of life.

Also, every excess in the human body slows the person down. Thus, there can never be a total turn around without a total clean-up. There are many factors with the capacity to slow one's down and the earlier you discover this, the better. God's plan for our lives is to make progress in all facets of life.

However, remember you don't stumble into greatness, you prepare for it. Total clean-up is part of the preparation for greatness.

Is never too late for this clean-up to take place. I love the scriptures that say old things have passed away and you have become a new creature. Any old conduct, character, activity, that can damage your brand has to be done away with before the next move of life.

You cannot build on any foundation that is faulty.

Total clean-up cannot have a positive effect without relating to positive-minded people and many more.

A man that pays a deaf ear to the cry of his inner mind need a total clean-up and until this happens, the living standard of the person will not be ameliorated. For instance, if the liver in a body system is bad, the whole body will suffer except something is done. You can't experience a total turn around when your mind is not renewed hence, I recommend a total clean-up as a solution to the menace. Friends, you have dwelt for too long in that situation, find out why you are still there because it's time to move to the next level.

You Will Never Be Better, Or Greater Than The Circle You Belong To.

So, it logically follows that to become better in life, you must always seek to upgrade your circle.

Let me sound a note of warning, l am not advocating the idea that some people have which makes them refuse to work, but instead seek to join some social organizations which they think will help them. A circle is like a fence; it only keeps bad people out, you must use it to keep good people in also. You will only attract to yourself those who are like you. So, seek to be a better person first.

The journey of life is from one circle to the other. Those who have the desire to be better must continually seek to surround themselves with people who will encourage them to get better.

You have to clean-up your circle. Anyone not having a progressive mind will always draw you backward.

Remember this adage: Show me your friend and I will tell who you are.

Remember, life is a mystery and it takes a man that is armed with the revelation to comprehend the essence of life.

Revelation plus a total clean-up give you a total turn around. A life without revelation suffers set back. It takes a revelation to comprehend the essence of a total clean-up.

Thus, the impact is made by men of uncommon revelation and to join these front liners, get set for a total turn around. Don't forget that the essence of life is beyond eating and drinking.

When you experience a turnaround, those around you will be blessed too. There was a country in the continent of Africa whose citizens were suffering from hunger, rejection, and sickness due to poor leadership. Amid this menace, a young man conceived a revelation on the need to clean the system in order for the people to experience a total turnaround. When he consequently sanitized the system, the nation experienced an economic boom (a total turnaround).

God is not through with you, there are things he wants you to clean out of your system in order to step to the next level of life.

"And in those times, there was no peace to him that went out, no to him that came in, but great vexations were upon all the inhabitants of the countries".

Israel suffered defeat, lack of people and hunger for a long time. There were some factors that were needed to be cleaned and these include lies, idolatry, and others. These sins could not allow them to draw closer to God and being far from God, the possibility of prosperity was not there but when they in their affliction purged themselves from these, there was a turnaround in all ramifications.

You can experience a turnaround with your willingness for a total clean-up. A nation that has forsaken God will pay dearly for it. I'm optimistic that your life will move from minimum to maximum when a total clean-up is in view.

Effectiveness of the Word

The effectiveness of the word cannot be overemphasized considering how men of old went from poverty to riches, from failure to success through the effectiveness of the word. The word that brings a solution to problems is not the word you know but the word you know and also apply.

Your understanding of God's word will purge you from negative minded persons whose aim is to get you distracted from God's plan in your life. This is so because the success of a man is attached to God's plan.

When your detractors succeed in detaching you from his plans the possibility of a turnaround remains impossible. Your addiction to God's word helps you to discern who to hang out with. The kind of people you relate with can influence your life to a certain degree. A wise man once said show me your friend and I will tell you who you are.

Therefore, the wrong association is one of the factors that should be purged out of your life but it will take an understanding of the word to do so.

When you keep relating to the wrong people, wrong things keep happening around you and this calls for a total clean-up.

The day right people walk into your life, you will experience a higher degree turnaround.

A young talented singer wasted his time hanging around those who neither had a future or the determination to secure one for themselves. In the course of this ungodly and ugly relationship, he discovered from the scriptures that evil communication corrupt good manner thereby purged him from this association.

A few months later he met the right people who were able to add value to his life and today, the young man is a music icon, a turnaround is possible.

There is a success strain in your DNA, purge yourself adequately through the knowledge of the word of God and become the star of your dream.

Purge Yourself from Negative Confession

Negative confession is a spirit with the capacity to thwart one's destiny if nothing is done about it. Men/women of old who had a total turnaround were armed with all are possible mentalities and a positive confession. Hence some could move from zero to being hero meanwhile it's pertinent to understand the fact that what you say, is what you become.

Until there is a total clean-up on your daily confession, a turnaround can't be in view.

Thus, we should be extremely careful about what we say to ourselves.

You can't confess poverty and expect to be rich, no. In view of this, I want to submit to you that it takes a man with an all is possibility mentality to maintain a positive confession. The Israelites were instructed to march down to Canaan and possess the land, the men with negative confessions died on the way, while the men with the all is the possible mentality, coupled with positive confession succeeded, and consequently experienced a total turnaround. What do you say to yourself on a daily basis?

Do not focus on your inabilities, instead, trust God's abilities always. It's time to examine yourself thoroughly and detect those factors that are capable to ruin your chances of moving to the next level.

A certain woman named Naomi experienced bitterness in her life to a point where she told the people to address her as "MARA" meaning bitterness. Her bitterness experience blinded her spiritual eyes thereby compelling her to talk negatively.

When situations are compelling you to talk negative, resist such a compelling force and learn to talk your way to victory no situation comes to destroy you but to make you strong both spiritually and physically.

Consequently, Naomi realized herself and changed her confession and helpers located her.

Purge yourself from all ungodliness and you will never regret you did.

Total clean-up will put you on a part of the total victory in life but just be aware that it will come with a cost at the beginning.

I give you this story about a lady who decided to forsake her wayward life of prostitution.

She went through so many troubles as all the free money that comes from every patron dried up.

So, it is for anyone who quits from illegal activities, there will be initial starvation that needs to be overcome.

But be rest assured as you build your new brand, people will begin to trust you, and your victory will become immeasurable.

This is our story; we have to rebrand by getting out of anything in our past that is a distraction.

In the initial stages, it can be tough but you will come out triumphantly.

5: Seed Gathering

This is one chapter I want you to pay much attention to if you really want to make it to the top.

What is the meaning of seed? The unit of reproduction of a flowering plant, capable of developing into another such plant.

Capable of developing into another such plant, is our focus here. For you to succeed you must have the capacity to multiply your seed.

Firstly, how do we get our seed before the multiplication process? Many have made so many mistakes in this area.

Every farmer knows that the most important factor in their success in business is their seeds, the same is applicable to any business or venture in life.

Every farmer will put away seeds for the next planting season to guarantee continuity of his produce.

Same must be seen with anyone who truly wants to succeed in life.

The first money you make in life is a seed that you must keep. You have to be willing to put away that vital money in a safe place as a seed to be planted.

Many people struggle throughout their lives paying one debt or the other because they did not have the seeds to sow.

Quick life experience story.

There is this friend of mine when we started a business in Nigeria in the late 90s.

As we progressed, everyone within our business circle was busy buying cars, building houses without any meaningful plan to stack some seed away.

This friend of mine refused to do all these things that we saw as a way to show that you have arrived financially.

He kept his money in a popular bank then in Nigeria. Many will taunt him, make jess of him, we saw him then as a timid person.

Many never knew then that he was saving his seed for sowing for tomorrow harvest.

With the power of his seed he was able to negotiate a deal with his bank to give him a guaranteed contract, today he is one of the richest young men in Africa.

The first thing you must do as you start is to create a seed. That can be invested for tomorrow.

Your seed in your business is your equity, it will give you the power to negotiate and it makes partners trust you.

Asking for arms and borrowing is one quickest way to frustrate you in life.

Yunus cites the oft-quoted statistic that one per cent of the population of rich countries owns 99% of the wealth. "And every day it's getting worse," he says. His radical idea, established in poverty-stricken Bangladesh in the 1970s, was that if poor people were given a proper start and encouragement, their natural entrepreneurship would flourish.

This is where I want you to reflect on how you really want to go in your life. With the seed you can gather you can become an entrepreneur, given the opportunity to create jobs and becoming an employer of labor like my friend I gave the brief story, today he employs thousands of people all over the country of Nigeria.

For every harvest there have to be a seed sown. Do not fall into the temptation of quick lone been paraded all around. They might just be a trap from the pit of hell.Many have gone that route and never recovered. What so ever you will buy on credit is always priced higher.

Borrowing results in bondage to creditors.

The very nature of going into debt is **entanglement**. It can take away your peace of mind to operate.

Seed gathering can help you to avoid all this entanglement and the false hope that it brings.

Borrowing is based on the assumption that **future conditions** will allow us to repay the debt which may not be there.

God did not want to come back after every dry season and cause new grass to grow; to avoid that He made sure within every tree that grows there has to be a seed.

God did not have to come and speak to the earth again for it to bring forth a different vegetation. Within the trees that the earth brought forth, there was a seed which is now producing the trees we see today.

God is at rest simply because He managed to assign every tree that grows to carry within itself a seed that produces the next generation of trees. Everything God created is busy multiplying itself. He created man and placed a seed inside him and told him to multiply and fill the earth. God does not ask you to multiply without Him giving you a seed that can multiply.

God gives you the power, grace and anointing to multiply. It is right inside of you. There is a principle you have to understand. The future you desire to have right now is demanding a seed that you have in the present. We sow seeds for the future we desire; the future you are praying for, hoping for and want to have is asking for a seed that you have in the present.

The seed you gathered is what guarantees your continued harvest. Do not eat the seed - sow it.

6: Understanding True Success

Many schools of thought have given different definitions of success. As a matter of fact, there is a misconception regarding this subject hence it's imperative for me to use this medium to throw more light on this subject in order to correct this misconception.

Some have seen success from the perspective of having so much money in the bank, not knowing one can have money without being successful.

Some people measure success from the scale of material possession unfortunately, it's beyond that. Success means finishing well in any choosing endeavor, and it begins from having a solid relationship with God; a man that has the fear of God is already successful. The fear of God is the beginning of wisdom which guarantees a right living that leads to true success. When you're successful spiritually, you will be successful physically.

In view of what I have demystified so far, who is a successful man?

A successful man can be described as one that has

known God, has a genuine source of income, takes pleasure in the prosperity of others, not easily give up, stands when others have fallen, a man with a possibility mentality and not egocentric in reasoning.

Understanding what true success is will lead you in the right part of life.

Without a true understanding of what success is you can easily be carried away with the wind of life.

The successful man

A successful person is usually armed with a possibility mentality and anyone who claimed to be successful without putting a smile on the face of the less privileged is poor. This is so because the success of a man is supposed to reflect on the people around him.

Meanwhile, some people have gotten their monies through dubious means, bought cars and houses and folks rate them as being successful. Anyone whose source of money is questionable is not a success despite all his material possessions.

Your source of success has to be transparent and traceable.

Aliko Dangote is a legitimate successful Nigerian

business magnate, investor and owner of the Dangote group with an estimate worth us$10.6 million. He has given succour to millions of people in Africa. The objective of a successful man is to add value to lives not to devalue them, this is what Mr Dangote is doing and his source of money is verifiable.

Some people have stolen government money and built themselves empires and as result parade themselves as successful people. Real successful people rose to the peak of their destiny through labor. Dangote group has employed thousands of Nigerians thereby making them outstanding in all facets of life.

We have financial and business success. Political success, science, sport, art or culture. Jay Jay Okocha retired as a successful footballer. He was successful because he finished well. To be in the list of successful men/women in our world, you must finish well. Thus, true success is the ability to finish well. Many took football as their career but couldn't finish well.

Some of the factors that can help an individual finish well and come out a success are:

Passion

Optimism

Focus and

Determination

The same thing that made others fall couldn't bring down others because they were optimistic, focused and determined. A successful person is someone with the courage to face challenges of life and come out eventually. A successful person is someone that has refused to take no for an answer.

Abraham Lincoln was an American statesman, politician, and a lawyer who served as the 16th American president of the United States.

He contested an election severally and failed but refused to quit. He had a possibility mentality hence he persisted and consequently, he became the 16th American president, he was a success.

Every successful person has a story behind his/her

glory.

But understand the fact that success is beyond what most people think.

Ways to Becoming Successful:
Hard work

You can't be successful overnight; it's a process that requires preparation and hard work.

A lot of people believe in cutting corners in order to be successful but this not right. To be successful in life, hard work must be in view. Hard work is needed regardless of your area of discipline. A medical doctor that is hard working will someday be a success. If he/she is a surgeon, he will be having successful operations without complication due to hard work and diligent.

Hard-working footballers are bound to be successful scoring goals or manning wings effectively.

Some folks have resolved into scam due to the fact that they are not ready to pay the price called "hard work".

Relate with success minded people

Relating with success-minded people is a sure way to becoming a success in your chosen career. Don't hate successful people because what you hate can't be attracted to you.

7: Becoming a Disciple with Distinction

A disciple is a follower of a superior being. In ensuring there is a turnaround, one is expected to follow his/her superior in the spirit of sincerity in order to be distinguished from others. When the Queen of Sheba visited King Solomon, the servants (disciples) of Solomon beginning from their dress code to mannerism, there was no compares. Every disciple that is loyal to the Master will unquestionably experience a total turnaround. It takes a disciple's heart to move to the next level in life.

There were many servants (disciples) in the days of King Solomon and the questions are why were his servants distinguished from others. It could be that Solomon's servants were passionate about their future hence they gave up everything and followed their master to a point where they stood out financially above their equals.

Avoid Gehazi's pitfall
The mercy of God chose Gehazi to be a disciple of prophet Elisha which means he was ordained to succeed

him but due to greed he fell from this exalted position to a nobody in all ramifications. Many disciples have fallen flat into the pit of Gehazi. We will check thoroughly those factors that can get you distinguished from others.

Seeing what God is seeing

Until a disciple grows to a point where he/she can see what God is seeing your chances of entering into the realm of a total turnaround can't be possible. The spiritual eyes of Gehazi were closed that's why he couldn't see the weight of his future. It takes spiritual mindedness to see what God is seeing.

To be a disciple with distinctions, visualize where you are going clearly and completely. Your ability to see where you are going will keep your focus and determination.

God is looking for disciples with spiritual understanding. During the earthly ministry of Jesus, about seventy disciples decided to follow him and in the process of time, they left due to some inconsequential reasons. In discipleship total obedience is what brings a total turnaround. These disciples left Jesus and fell into the pit of Gehazi because their spiritual eyes were closed.

Comparing

Comparing is a spirit and when it comes, one can fall off track. To succeed as a disciple, avoid the spirit of comparing. Many gospel preachers have compromised their faiths in quest of trying to be like someone else. We get rewarded when we avoid comparing yourself to others and focus on Him that has called us from darkness into his marvelous light.

Righteousness is doing the right things irrespective of what our neighbor is doing. God's plan is to lift you to a greater height in life but you need to be focused and consistent. Perhaps Judas Iscariot wanted to be like others hence he sold his master for thirty pieces of silver and doomed his life. Friends, you can be a disciple with distinction, it's a matter of choice.

Make a choice now!

Being a disciple with distinction is a function of choice. The choice you make in life is very vital and entering into the realm of 360 degrees is a function of choice. The choice you make today determines how your tomorrow will be. Thus, it's essential for someone to be careful when it comes to choosing to make.

Your steps in life are as a result of the choice you have made. Let me use this medium to announce to you that poverty is a choice and prosperity is a choice too.

Your actions are determined by your choice. Don't look for an accidental turnaround because a turnaround is in phases and your choice and action qualify you for the next phase. Abraham was a disciple in his time. He made a choice to follow God sincerely despite his predicament. Some would have seen the choice of Abraham as a display of foolishness and mediocrity.

To Abraham, in his choice to follow God unconditionally was a preparation for the next level. The choice of Abraham resulted in his name be written in gold. Meanwhile, the father of Abraham Tera died a nobody due to the fact that he couldn't do any outstanding thing or gave himself as a disciple. Your outstanding performances are what graduate you to outstanding turn around.

The choice of Abraham gave him an edge over others and consequently save his generation from hardship. The height his father couldn't attain, Abraham attained through the choice he made. The limitation was broken and a door of a total turnaround opened unto him. Everyone who had their names written in the scriptures did outstanding things either negatively or positively, a choice has the capacity to distinguish you from others.

A disciple with distinction does not take no for an answer. To him (a disciple with distinction) every problem has a solution.

Focus

This is the quality of giving concentration or attention to your assignment. When your assignment lacks focus, failure will be inevitable. Abraham (as a disciple) was focused on his assignment hence he succeeded. Though he was old, the scripture records that he prospered in all things.

When a disciple loses focus from his assignment, Satan and failure become his focus. The truth of the matter is the devil will do everything within his powers to get us distracted because he knows when we are focused that we will experience a higher degree of a turn around that is why we need to resist him with all that is in us.

Do not let the devil distract you from your focus. Apostle Paul faced uncountable distractions, yet he remained focus moving from one level to another.

There are various ways with which the devil would want to get you distracted and these could be (a) sickness (b) disappointment (c) lack or (d) bareness.

In all of the above, we are more than conquerors.

Therefore, stay focused in order to experience a higher degree of a turnaround.

Hard work

Hard work is one of the qualities of a disciple aiming at distinction. Discipleship is not a license for hardship. If Jesus could work hard, we should work hard too, there is no place for laziness in this kingdom. When a disciple does not have "hard work" in his vocabulary, a non-disciple will prosper while the disciple will remain in the valley of pity.

History has proven that a lot of people who succeeded did so not just based on the grace of God, but hard work contributed a great percentage to their success. It's now time to shun laziness in order to stand out.

Abraham worked hard. Isaac worked hard and King David worked hard.

The spirit of hard work is what wakes you up in the morning to pray, evangelize and scan your environment for a new opportunity.

That you are a follower of God does not mean you should look for pity, sick or poor. We deserve the best. The world today is run by hard thinkers and hardworking people. Our faith does not promote laziness therefore; wake up from your slumber in order to take your rightful place in the kingdom.

They that are asleep can't experience a total turnaround, only those who are awake. Hence, I charge you to get into your redemptive position in life from now.

8: Do Not Rest on Yesterday's Victory

Work to ensuring a continuity victory over lack, frustration, and setback.

Many have experienced a turnaround but after some time, they fell down flat from where they started from. A turnaround must be maintained if one truly wants to remain at the peak of destiny. That you succeeded yesterday does not mean you should go to sleep. Men that go to sleep due to a little breakthrough will live to regret it. It's imperative to strive to get better every day. Your today's turn around may not be enough to sustain you tomorrow, be wise.

This reminds me of a hard-working young man who got a nice job after his university education. With time he bought a building in the city and had a beautiful car. But he failed to realize that it will get to a stage in his life where his salary won't be enough to care for him and his family.

Life is in phases, what seems to be a turning point today may not sustain you tomorrow and that's where intelligence is applied.

Every phase has its challenges or responsibilities. The

guy whose story I narrated above eventually got married with children and years later he realized his salary couldn't solve his family challenges.

He suffered because he rested on the little victory he had over poverty as a bachelor and thought that was how it will continue.

This is the problem of so many people, hence some could laugh yesterday and cry a day after because they failed in their responsibilities. Thus, a turnaround can be planned for.

Save/Invest

It's not enough to earn money, wisdom demands you save it for future advancement. If you had made millions of dollars yesterday and you didn't save it, then be prepared to battle poverty in the future because a turnaround can't be in view.

It's not how much you earn but how you are able to save is what matters. A lot of people were very rich yesterday but extremely poor today because certain principles of life were not observed. We have seen families who are able to pass a high degree turnaround mentality to generation unborn thereby making them strong and the younger generation not depending on yesterday's victory of their parents. They are always ready to work hard and save for rainy days so as to ensure continuity.

Meanwhile, money in your account can't make you a superstar until it's invested wisely. Through a positive investment, there can be a turnaround. Take advantage of your victory over lack yesterday and invest in something meaningful today. However, do not invest in an area you have no knowledge about.

Money on its own can't make you rich until it's invested wisely.

If you're aspiring to get to the climax of your destiny, then be mindful of what I have demystified. Every investment is determined by the availability of cash, remember what you start small will be big in due time. Information at your possession goes a long way to determining how effective you can be as an investor. Ask the richest businessman in Africa and he will tell you the essence of investment and the danger of resting on your yesterday's victory. Business-minded people know the information is potent enough to ensure their turn around.

Therefore, save that money, invest that money and become a front- liner in the kingdom.

Don't be myopic

One of the factors that have made some people rest in yesterday's victory is their inability to see far in life.

The level of any person placement in life is determined by far the person can see. Some were comfortable with one room apartment forgetting that kids will be born to the family.

Some were contented with 100 dollar's job without the knowledge that with time the money will no longer be meaningful. A lot of people have missed their today because they allowed their yesterday's victory to get them intoxicated.

Centuries ago in some part of Africa, children that were loved by parents were not allowed to go to school. Their duties were to eat and sleep because their parents were illiterate and eventually truncated the future of these kids, don't be myopic.

Satan wants to fight back

A turnaround is not limited to financial breakthrough, it

goes beyond that. Each time a battle is won it means a turnaround has taken place.

When a person recovers from sickness, a turnaround has taken place. When closed doors are open and connections reactivated, that means turnarounds have taken place. Prophet Elijah killed four hundred prophets of Baal which were a huge victory. The following day, Jezebel threatened Elijah with death and perhaps Elijah felt relax after his victory over Baal's prophets hence he became afraid when he received the message.

That you prayed yesterday and had an open door does not mean you should relax. Satan hardly gives up, he wants to fight back. Perhaps Elijah would have gotten a major victory if he had withstood the threat of Jezebel. Satan searches for an opportunity to fight and that is why anyone that lives based on the past victory is either under Satanic attack or he is ignorant.

We have heard people say "I remember when I used to be very rich". The question is, what did you do with the money?

Be prudent in your doing; don't create an avenue for Satan to fight and the future belong to those who managed their yesterday wisely.

9: From Instruction to A Turnaround

Most people who experienced a turnaround in the days were due to instructions they obeyed. Proud people do not obey instructions and this is one of the reasons people in this category hardly succeed. When God is set to lift a man from one level to another, he gives instructions. The success of God's people is determined by their willingness to obey instructions.

God's instructions may look foolish from humans' perspectives but if one is humble enough to obey, you will be amazed to discover what you have been praying for. In our journey to a sweatless life, let's ensure we obey every instruction from God.

You have struggled for too long; this is the set time to be announced by God.

Before the miracle

Jesus attended a marriage ceremony and, in the process, the wine finished. I want to believe the celebrant was already tensed unknowingly to him that there will be a turnaround. What Jesus did was to give an instruction. Meanwhile, Mary the mother of Jesus had advised his disciples to obey whatever instructions from Jesus. Consequently, his disciples filled the empty jars with water and Jesus turned it to wine. The miracle happened because his disciples obeyed. Who told you an insignificant can't be blessed? With God, all things are possible. He that is rejected and abandoned by men can become a testimony when willing to obey instructions.

A scenario where wine got finished in a ceremony of that magnitude was shameful and I believe there were mockers waiting to see the outcome but Christ disappointed them.

Friends, life can be sweet when obedience to instructions is applied. A man got a job offer abroad, the salary was encouraging. The establishment offered to pay for his ticket and others. In the midst of this, he got instruction on what to do but he refused due to pride hence he lost the offer.

Disobedience to instructions has delayed many destinies, closed many doors and disgraced many persons, obedience is better than sacrifice. Abraham was instructed to offer Isaac as a sacrifice and without questions, he obeyed and that made him a success.

The yoke of a generational curse was broken by

Abraham through obedience to instructions. Whatever God has instructed you to do, go ahead and do it, to experience a high degree turn around. Before Abraham died, he left gifts (riches) to his sons because God had prospered him. Your obedience to God's instruction will not only be a blessing to you but to your generation as well. When Abraham died, Isaac built his life from what his dad left behind. It's wrong for a man to die leaving nothing for the family. Listen to God's instructions and your generation unborn will never suffer. Research has shown that some children whose parent were firmly established succeeded based on what their parents left behind. You can't be adamant to God's instructions and expect to be blessed like Abraham, no.

Enforce a total turnaround

A woman whose husband died poor and left some debt behind did something commendable. She ran to Prophet Elisha for a total turnaround when creditors came to take her children for slavery. When she obeyed instructions given to her by Elisha, she became oil marketer.

God is in interested in your turnaround. Our

suffering does not glorify him in any way. Therefore, make up your mind to obey whatever the scripture says. The history of your family can be written again when God has finished with what he is doing in your life.

Failure is not in the lineage of God's people because God can't fail and so neither can you. Except you are not born again, failure is not permitted to touch you. This is your season to experience a total turnaround in your life, get ready to obey instructions from the master through the scripture. The widow became a blessing to people around her when she obeyed. God is still raising those that are obeying his instructions.

Saul's kind of people

Saul was ordained king in Israel from the tribe of Benjamin. His tribe was the least, yet God chose him. Many a time when God wants to lift a man to a higher degree in life, he does not put your family antecedents into consideration. The first instruction was for him to wait for seven days until (he) Samuel arrives. The establishment of his kingdom was to be determined by this instruction. The failure of a man begins the very day he believes he has arrived. With this mentality, instruction will not be regarded as anything useful. King Saul was given a second

Chance but he messed it up also. May you never miss your opportunity in life. Thus, in this kingdom, your graduation to the next level of a turnaround is attached to instruction.

Find out what God has instructed you to do, that's the vehicle to the peak of your destiny.

10: Breaking the Wings of Fault Finders

Atrocities caused by fault finders cannot be overemphasized. Many destinies have been aborted due to activities of fault finders.

Many marriages, churches, and others are in shamble as a result of fault finders. Their objective is to destroy lives because they are Satanic agents positioned in strategic places to cause havoc. Until their wings are broken, you may not be able to experience a high degree of turn around. Many a time they make you feel inferior through their utterances.

They focus on your weakness instead of the area of your strength thereby compelling you to believe your God is incapable in all ramifications. But if their wings are broken, you march into the next level of a total turn around.

Jesus healed a man on a Sabbath day, the Jews (fault finders) found fault with that. Their aim was to stop Jesus through the weapon of discouragement. They knew where Jesus was heading to hence, they became tools in the hand of the devil.

Fault finders in marriages

Mutual trust is spiritual gasoline with the capability of getting any marriage work. Any marriage that works on this basis is on her way to a positive turn around. Therefore, when mutual trust is lacking due to activities of fault finders, the possibility of the marriage to enjoy a total turn around can't be in view. Trust is one of the spiritual components that lifts any marriage from lack to abundance of favor, joy, and prosperity.

If one is not careful enough, you may allow the arrow of fault finders to penetrate your home and when this happens, you experience marriage break up thereby fulfilling the wish of the enemy. It is prudent to trust your spouse regardless of the circumstance in order to enjoy the blessing attached by God.

There is no perfect marriage anywhere in the world, every marriage has its ups and downs, yours is not special. Your spouse can be accused with the intention of destroying your home. Friends, wake up and add value to your marriage and don't allow a third party in your marriage. When mutual trust and respect is lacking in any relationship, it gives the devil the legal right to fight but you can stop him through wisdom and understanding.

Bluff them

When they tell you that your spouse did this and that, bluff them and walk away and by so doing you will unquestionably walk in the realm of favors.

In trying to respond to all the accusations leveled against your spouse may ruin your home.

Jesus was accused of so many things and he bluffed them. What you do not cherish will be despised by people around.

In order to witness a high degree of a turnaround in your home, bluff the accusers and place value on your relationship.

Their activities in the church

Activities of fault finders have hindered the growth of many churches. They specialized in criticizing all the moves of the pastor, reading negative meanings to his prayer points, his preaching's and consequently rob themselves the opportunity of living a blessed life because the anointing you do not value can't be a blessing to you. Many have ignorantly dug their early graves, created an avenue for lack and frustration through this menace. They are out to destroy the pastor and the church but Jesus said I will build my church and the gate of hell shall not prevail against it. Any person that wants to succeed must ensure he bluff them, if not it will degenerate to discouragement.

Discouragement births frustration and frustration births destruction. Nehemiah was raised by God to rebuild the broken walls of Jerusalem (a type of a church) and fault finders rose from all angles with a view to stopping him from succeeding If you want to please people, you end up displeasing God. The right thing to do is to remain resilient and focused. Sanballat and Tobias rose up against Nehemiah as to weaken his hands from the building but failed and Nehemiah succeeded and finally entered into a new level of life. Your success is attached to what God has called you to do.

To enter into a better tomorrow, handle your assignment prudently. There is no excuse for your failure. You have what it takes to place your detractors where they belong and hold onto your vision.

Many successful people crossed many hurdles before

they got to their destinations. As a minister of the gospel, understand the fact that behind every glory, there is a story. Nehemiah stood his ground not minding what fault finders were busy doing because he was passionate about his assignment.

That church under your supervision can't die, God knows how to silence fault finders just as he did in the time of Nehemiah, David, Moses, and Abraham.

Prayers

We do not wrestle against flesh and blood but against principalities and powers.

As stated earlier, their aim is to stop you from seeing the open door, fruitfulness and so on. There is a spirit behind the activities of these guys and one of the ways out is to arrest them through prayers. It's the spiritual that controls the physical. Any advancement you can't make in the spiritual can't be made in the physical.

Therefore, your next level of turnaround begins in the spiritual.

A praying church is a dominion church regardless of the oppression of fault finders. More so, a praying person is bound to experience a higher degree of blessing in life.

Acts of the Apostles recorded how King Herod died and the church multiplied. Herod was a type of oppressor and a fault finder with the aim of hindering the church from prospering.

But when the church prayed, his mouth was closed forever and the church grew in all areas.

When the mouth of your detractors is closed, there shall be open doors. You are destined to break their wings through prayers. Prayer is a weapon with the capability to do what is humanly unimaginable, I see you succeed where others have failed.

11: Dangers of Unnecessary Worries

The term "worry" is the state of being troubled or giving way to mental anxiety.

Worries are a fact of life. Most time when your expectations are not met, you get worried. Every person on the surface of the earth gets worried at one point or the other.

However, worries sometimes can create a platform through which you experience a breakthrough. Some persons may be sleeping without activating their mental potency with a view of ensuring a successful future.

But in this chapter, we will be dealing with unnecessary worries. This is based on the fact that there are worries that are unquestionably unnecessary in all areas.

40% of our worries are issues that can never come to pass. Worry births anxiety and anxiety create depression and depression is a killer by virtue of research. Worries sends signal of messages that are not even available anywhere. No man makes progress in an atmosphere of worries. Worries weaken a man and when this happens, the person's future can be thwarted if a good care is not taken.

Many have met their untimely death due to unnecessary worry.

Distraction

Every successful future is built with the tool of concentration but if worries are given a chance, distractions become the order of the day. No one succeeds in the midst of distraction. It takes concentration to build a nation, business or any chosen career. A certain man had a dream of establishing a firm that could employ ten thousand workers and in the course of this, worries came in asked; (1) where will you get such a massive land for the project? (2) The project is capital intensive; how do you raise such money? With these questions, the young man broke down in doubt and confusion because he was distracted.

You can get to the peak of your destiny if you can fight distraction.

After some months, the young man came to his

senses, seeing his ability clearly and completely, no longer his inability as suggested worries, consequently he got his dream fulfilled.

Your dreams are achievable if you're ready to do the needful.

Courage

It takes courage to stand tall and not being a victim of unnecessary worries. One of the dangers of getting worried unnecessarily is non-achievement. Non-achievement is the state of not being able to accomplish any good in life.

Many have fallen into the pit of unnecessary worries due to lack of courage. Your situation may be so discouraging and you may be tempted to subject yourself to unnecessary worries but I'm telling you - be courageous.

It takes courage to take delivery of your destiny. Those that are courageous will ascend the throne of their glory. You are not an accidental discharge; resist the temptation of being unnecessarily worried.

Focus

Focus is the state of showing concentration or attention to what or where you are going. It takes determination to be focused. When determination is not in view, you become a prey of unnecessary worries.

There is a future in that career if you are focused enough. You are being criticized because they do not want you to be celebrated but if you remain focused and enthusiastic, only the sky can be your limit; there is a light at the end of the tunnel.

Check your association

Your association has the power to determine your destination to an extent. When you relate with positive-minded people, you walk in dominion and influence over worries. When you walk with people, right things start happening around you. Victims of unnecessary worries would want you to be part of their team thus; it's pertinent to check your association thoroughly.

Friends who are not conscious of their destination have no positive advice to give to you.

Jesus once told his disciples not to be fearful or worry. He knew the hazard of fear or unnecessary worries hence he brought them to his camp and those in his camp fulfilled their destinies except Judas.

Carefully locate a good association in order to be free from unnecessary worries.

Mr Clement narrated how he would have dropped out of the university if not for his good friends around. Through the effort of his good friends, he graduated as a medical doctor. Money is not everything; friends can help you see your ability in the face of adversity. If you are in the company of fearful people, you too will be fearful and worried unnecessarily.

Don't abort your future

Suicide is a major national public health issue in the United States of America. In 2016, there were 44,965 recorded.

The suicide rate among Americans age 35 to 64 increased by nearly 30 per cent. Most of these victims had dreams but terminated their future due to unnecessary worries.

Suicide is condemnable regardless the reason. Unnecessary worries are one of the reasons for suicide. Take a stroll to a cemetery and about 75 percent of persons laying there died unfulfilled. The sooner you come to understand that worries can't increase your status, the better.

This is no longer in America alone but a world problem. There cannot be a turnaround in the grave, let worries drive you to a positive move, setting goals, going after them and wait as the light come to shine on you.

Deal with worries positively and avoid anyone that is unnecessary.

12: Surviving in a Two World Order

To survive is to live, to remain alive or to live past a life-threatening event. Basically, there are two orders on earth, good, evil, light, darkness poverty and riches. It's important you know how to survive in this two-world order.

The fact is that you can't reach out to this two-world order at the same time. Each of these orders has its principles and one's obedience to its principle determines whether one's riches will be durable or not,

In quest of trying to survive, some have embraced darkness instead of light, bad instead of good and so on

This chapter is an eye-opener to those who have made mistake in the course of yearning for a total turn around and those who are on the queue to fall prey of this same menace. It's one thing to know there are two world orders and it's another thing to device a means to ensuring that you survive in the midst of this.

Riches can be deceitful

Deceitfulness of riches cannot be overemphasized. Many have sold their souls to Satan in the name of money. Like they say; if you can't beat them you join them. Remember you can be rich through a positive means.

Greed

Greed is an excessive desire for more than the needful or deserved, especially of money, wealth, food or other possession.

In the course of my research in order to know reasons some person's intentionally embraced darkness instead of light, I have discovered greed as one of the reasons.

Though it's said that human's wants are insatiable but some schools of taught teach about godly contentment. A greedy person can go any length not minding the consequent to get whatever he wants.

Greediness has led many astray. I'm seeing greediness as a spirit thus; greedy people would continue to be greedy no matter how riches they have acquired.

Identify them and separate yourself

Like they say, "birds of a feather flock together". Finding yourself in the midst of greedy people can influence you to a point of behaving like them. To be on the safer side is for you to identify them and separate yourself immediately, wisdom is profitable to direct.

Judas was greedy and egocentric in all ramifications. In his quest for money, he went as far as betraying his master and had the money he needed but was not alive to enjoy it.

Friends the wages of sin is death. I know of a man that was denied a political position since he refused to join his colleagues in darkness, lies and evil.

Be success-minded

Success mindedness will activate something inside of you that won't accept failure as the final answer. It will help you to see differently, act differently and relate differently.

Laziness

Most people misfortune is traceable to laziness. No one succeed overnight, it takes a preparation to get there. Some persons lack preparation in their vocabulary hence they find it difficult to survive through a legitimate means. There is no future for those that are lazy, heaven help those that help themselves.

Therefore, laziness is another reason some people chose lies, darkness and evil. Make sure you scan your environment and find something meaningful to do.

Men from the other world order can't give you a helping hand except you join them. Don't allow laziness ruin your future. If you failed yesterday, strategize and go back. There is great chance that you will succeed this time.

Decision

This can be seen as firmness of conviction. One's decision shows how mature the person is, maturity is not in age, age is a number. Men that are indecisive can't survive in this world. Make a decision today and abide by it, success and failure are matters of decision.

Your decision today determines what happens tomorrow.

13: It All Begins With Questioning

A lot of people are strategically positioned to destroy destinies. Most of them are in disguised of good friends but inwardly they are Satan reincarnate. We are in the last days hence a lot of things that are beyond human understanding; happening and these happenings have served as a deterrent to others.

One good day, Satan walked into the garden and asked, "Did God really told you not to eat of this fruit?" there are questions that are capable of making you to doubt the Godly instructions you received from God or your ability to succeed in life.

I enjoin you not to distracted to every question. Eve lost her place of honor due to her inability not to say no to questions thrown to her by Satan.

These questions in the garden were optional; Eve was not under duress to respond to any of the questions. When your ears are opened to lies or inconsequential questions, your faith gets weaken and you start seeing yourself from the perspective of a loser.

Doubt is a killer

Through questions from Satan, Eve doubted Adam, her husband, doubted God and her future. The essence of questioning Eve was to ruin her future and he succeeded because she gave him attention.

In this two-world order, another reason young men and women embrace lies instead of truth is because they have doubted their future.

This could be as a result of questions Satanic agents have thrown to them. These agents do not come to say they want to destroy, but if you are sensitive enough, you will understand their gimmick.

Believe in yourself

You cannot make an impact until you believe in yourself; there is an inner ability in you. The enemy only points out the weakness and asked if you can still succeed based on this. Self-believe is a weapon that would give your enemy a technical knockout, this is what Eve lacked in the garden.

Your dreams can be fulfilled through self-believe. You are a divine and perfect project in the hand of almighty and with self-believe, you can go places.

It is time to shun them

What you hear can determine whether you will continue, in pursuit of your dreams or not. In order not to allow the negative happen, shun them now; don't hang around negative information carriers.

Their aims are to kill, steal and destroy. What you entertain has the power to strengthen or weaken you, be careful!

Tactics

We live in a battlefield called life and you must understand the tactics of the enemy to win in the warfare. The devil has changed its tactics of war and many are still making a big mistake chasing Satan as a roaring lion that he was.

God has stripped him of that power, and now, he has worn his new cloth called subtle and devious.

Anything thing that makes you question what God said about you, just remember devious.

Devious people are crafty, clever, sly, deceitful and dishonest. They always think of ways to trip you that no one else would ever think of.

Questioning what God said was the first trick Satan

pulled on humanity and it worked. Satan is careless about the pain and suffering he creates when you are separated from your maker, God. As God is working to get you in shape and track of life, the devil is working too to take you out of track.

The tactics today is the secret voices creeping into your mind every second, strange enough to put you on hold, to question if God really loves you, look at yourself, problems, mess everywhere, how can God say, He loved me and my life is still like this?

Until you learn to resist the devil, he will keep coming until you fall. All he wants is for you to question God. Say to the devil every time you hear these discouraging voices, shut up am not listening to your crap.

Imagine the difference, it could have made if Eve did not listen to the crap of the devil.

In life, the devil wants to mess up your mind, head and heart. Your secret weapon in this war of your soul is the name of JESUS. It works.

Satan is saying do not believe what the preacher is saying, can't you see am here for your interest, voices, voices and voices they will keep coming till the end of life. The devil never gives up, tell him to shut up.

Until you get your tactics right in any warfare, you are bound to lose.

Every war has its tactics and strategy, there are time you press forward and times you calm down to watch. Silent at times is a tactic, weighing the gain and the loss is a tactic.

Idleness and slothfulness breeds trouble, staying busy constructively is a tactic.

Keeping your eyes on the big ball, the ultimate goal of your life.

14: One Key to a Turn Around, Prayer

Everything in life that begins with prayers has a better chance to succeed but that is not the only factor that determined success.

Prayers is asking God to stand behind whatever you are doing for you to experience true peace of mind.

The excess of life is to have peace of mind in all that you do. The true meaning of a man that can truly be called success is the man that have peace of mind.

Wealth and influence does not guarantee the peace I am talking about.

There are many people who are wealthy with great influence in society. With their position, the one thing they crave for the most is peace. Nothing can buy that.

The most important treasure of mankind can only be gotten through prayers.

This book, 'my life my prayer' is a testimony of my family life.

In the story of our life, there were moments when it seems pointless to even pray, but by faith one thing keeps coming to our mind, there is God, we think about many things He has done in the past for us, what we have passed through because of prayers answered.

One thing that we will love to share with you is, not that there are no moments that we were not rattled, but there is always one thing, peace of mind.

Prayers create the peace that you need, to start again even when the world is against you.

In your journey in life there are many things that will stand as a stumbling block, never overestimate your position in life, the people you trusted the most can disappoint you, the job that you trusted so much, the health that has never failed you, the savings in the bank, name it.

Many have taken liberty for granted and no longer have time with God in prayers.

There is a great danger in liberty when it drives you to live independently out of God.

The devil has been so successful in driving many out the fellowship that existed between them and God, driving them to a never-ending list of pointless ambitions.

The creator has the ultimate right to the created and if the created need a fix, there is no better place to go for the fix but the creator.

Prayers create the atmosphere for the created and the creator to look at each other continually to avoid moments of disrepair.

Stepping back to our life, me and my wife. We met years ago and never knew she will be my wife one day.

She has prayed a prayer growing up as a young school girl. Lord, please give me a man that will help me to serve you.

Never knowing how, but to her the maker hears and the answer will come. Many years went by, there were relationships that were near to marriage but they never happened; Not by her making neither did she remember the prayers she has made to the all hearing God.

Remember the word peace of mind, anything thing that does not give you peace of mind, be wary about it.

She was not looking for a wealthy man as many young girls will do; 'someone that will help me serve God'.

Prayer brings your desire and goals to the Lord. He hears and He cares.

Now let us fast forward, we met again after a long time and in a very distressing time of my life. My father has just passed away, my hero, the one who always believe in me, he never judged me, always looking for every avenue for me to succeed, taught me how to respect everyone around me and love for all and hate for none.

The moment of thought, it was really a tough moment, and behold there she is saying to me do not worry everything will be ok. And we prayed. One thing I did not want to forget to tell you is that we were honest to each other.

I was honest to her about my situation as at then; that am going to be starting life afresh with nothing anywhere.

The days went by and the rest is now history, today we are celebrating our seven-year wedding anniversary with a testimony of a prayer answered; 'A man who will help me serve God'.

Today God has blessed us with beautiful children, God is supplying our needs and His praises fills our lips on a daily basis.

What are your prayers?

Early in life, you must identify this key and the most effective tool to live a successful life with peace of mind.

The prayers in this book is just a guide. Do not be limited by it and do not make it a ritual. Develop a personal relationship with God. Become a lover of God, if you make prayer your watch word, you will rule your world.

PRAYER POINTS

Marital Blessing

Meditation: Colossians 1: 9 – 10

Isaiah 54:17

Matthew 18:18

Revelation 13:10

Prayer Points

1. I bind and cancel every power militating against my family in Jesus name.

2. I plead the blood of Jesus upon our marriage and I declare our freedom in Jesus name.

3. I declare that the blessing attached to my marriage shall manifest.

4. I break and destroy every evil marriage covenant working against me in Jesus name.

5. Every mark of hatred put on my spouse to hate me; I curse you today in Jesus mighty name.

6. I declare the door of my marital blessing open today.

7. Shame will never be a portion of my marriage.

8. Every stranger in my marriage, pack your load and leave now.

9. The rain of the wicked will never fall on my marriage.

Breaking Barriers

Meditation: Psalms 121:4

Psalms 2:9

Isaiah 49:25

Prayer Points

1. Every foundational barrier on my way is destroyed.

2. God open my spiritual eyes to see the cause of my set-back and the solution.

3. I release stones against every force behind my barrier and I command the Satanic force to be silenced now.

4. According to your words, I am now a new creature thus loads of my fathers shall never locate me.

5. (Sing this spiritual song: Let my God arise... and my enemies are scattered) I break every bus/stop placed against my destiny.

6. Evil decisions holding down my miracle scatter.

7. Every executor of failure on my way, the Lord rebuke you in Jesus mighty name.

8   Every evil arrow targeting my glory catch fire in Jesus name.

9   I receive divine visitation that will put to an end all my barrier in Jesus name.

10 All strange association summoned against my downfall shall never prosper in Jesus name.

11 I lose myself from any kind of bondage declaring my body, spirit, and soul free in Jesus name.

Declare Promotion

Scriptural Reading: Psalms 75:6

Prayer Points

1   Let all my destiny helpers remember me today.

2   My departed glory be restored in Jesus name.

3   Promotion hunters will never terminate my promotion in Jesus name.

4   My captured promotion will be released now in Jesus name.

5   What demoted my parents will never demote me.

6   My finances shall increase and the works of my hands will experience a total turn around in Jesus name.

7   I arrest every demonic architect behind demotion in my life and family.

8   I release my promotion from any spiritual cage in Jesus mighty name.

9   Every demonic tree that has swallowed my promotion, vomit it now in Jesus name.

10. Every Satanic gathering whether in the air, water, forest, etc. whose arm is to bring me down. Today I command fire from above to consume you in Jesus mighty name.

Your Business Success

Scriptural Reading: Exodus 23:20

Prayer Points

1. Give God quality thanks for your life and business.

2. Confess every known and unknown sin to God.

3. Let all my doors of business opportunities open unto me.

4. Every demonic driver, driving my business backward catch fire in Jesus name.

5. Whatever that has stagnated business in my environment will never stagnant my own.

6. I speak to my business to begin to ring profit from this hour.

7. God revealed to me:
    a. The problem behind my business success
    b. The secret behind the business success
    c. How to take my business abroad

8. Satan takes your hands off my business success in Jesus name.

9. Let the anger of God fall on any devilish money pass to my business purse in Jesus mighty name.

10 Let all enemies of my business success be disgraced.

Freedom from Death

Scriptural Reading: Psalms 23:4

Prayer Points

1. Praise God for who he is and what he will do in your life.

2. I break the yoke of untimely death and I declare myself free.

3. Every arrow of death sent against my family members, catch fire in Jesus name.

4. I remove my name from the book of untimely death.

5. Every spiritual policeman assigned to arrest, break down and be confused in Jesus name.

6. By faith, I drink the blood of Jesus and I decree whatever that God has not planted in my system receive the fire of God in Jesus name.

7. Every darkness trying to cover my life, be removed in Jesus mighty name.

8. I declare, not my blood nor that of the members of my family.

9. God pursues every power that is pursuing my life.

10. I command every evil trap set against me to catch its owner in Jesus name.

Power Against Evil Dreams

Scriptural Reading: Isaiah 54:17

Psalms 125:3

2 Timothy 4:18

Prayer Points

1. Praise and worship God. Remember, the Lord inhabits the praise of His people.

2. I bind and chain down every spiritual attacker in Jesus mighty name.

3. Every demonic manipulation through my dream your time is over be destroyed permanently in Jesus mighty name.

4. I bind and cancel all spiritual load placed on my shoulder in the dream.

5. Every door through which Satan has been attacking me in the dream closed permanently in Jesus name.

6. I break and destroy every curse working against me in the dream.

7. All the defeat I have been suffering in the dream, be expired now in Jesus.

8   I command all my disgrace in the dream to turn to grace. All my shame turn to share. All my failures turn to success. All my demotion, turn to promotion, mention them.

9   All the test in my dream, turn to testimony.

10 All the close untimely death in my dream, turn to long life.

11 All the poverty in my dream, turn to prosperity in Jesus mighty name.

Overcoming Forces of Darkness Called Wasters

Scriptural Reading: Acts 10:38

John 14:23

Isaiah 62:22

Psalm 17:4

Prayer Points

1. Take-up a song of praise to God from your heart.

2. Confess and forsake all your sins.

3. I stand against the following in Jesus wonderful name.
    a. The power that wants to waste the labor of my hands
    b. The power that wastes destiny from succeeding the power of harvest consumers
    c. The power to labor like an elephant but eat like an ant.

4. Every household enemy that has caused many businesses to collapse, I declare my life and properties holy- Ghost zone.

5. God my coming to this world will never be a waste of time in Jesus name.

6   From this hour I shall reap the fruit of my labor.

7   I will never labor for another to come and reap.

8   I speak to the sun and the moon to favor me in Jesus name.

9   Every yoke of leaking pocket I destroy you in Jesus name.

10 Every serpent that wants to swallow the work of my hand, be disgraced in Jesus mighty name.

11 Every failure at the edge of a miracle, pack your load out of my life and family now in Jesus mighty name.

12 I command my city to favor me in all areas.

13 I refuse to labor in vain in Jesus mighty name.

Total Deliverance

Scriptural Reading: Gal. 6:27

Gal. 3:13

2 Corinthians 6::14

Prayer Points

1. Appreciate God for His powers to deliver and set free.

2. I declare deliverance on my finances.

3. I remove my name from the register of the evil ones in Jesus name.

4. I renounce my membership of any of the following: water spirit, witches and wizards, cultism, familiar spirit: mention them.

5. Jesus lay hand on me and deliver me completely.

6. Every property of Satan in my possession catch fire in Jesus mighty name.

7. I withdraw my picture from the altar of Satan in Jesus mighty name.

8. Every demonic mirror working against me, be broken.

9   Every idol crying against my peace and that of my family members be destroyed now in Jesus mighty name.

10 I withdraw any part of my body deposited on the altar of Satan (Mention them and pray: e.g. blood, legs, hand, etc.

11 Holy spirit fight and deliver me totally in Jesus mighty name.

Divine Favour

Scriptural Reading: Proverbs 21:1

Proverbs 11:27

Psalms 8:5

Prayer Points

1. Father make my business find favour before buyers.

2. God let me find favour before men and women.

3. Father make my name find favour heaves.

4. Powers that have stood against my favour these years, God let them stumble and fall in Jesus mighty name.

5. I command my money that was caged to be released now in Jesus name.

6. God put my matter in the hand of those whom you have raised to favour me.

7. Those you have assigned to favour me will never rest except they do so.

8. I call my destiny supporter from the North, East, South, and West to locate me in Jesus name.

9 I break the backbone of evil pursuer whose aim is to stop my favour from manifesting.

10 I stop the operations of fear in my life in Jesus name.

Place an Embargo Against Unwanted Happening

Scriptural Reading: Psalms 139:23

Prayer Points

1 I lose myself from conscious and unconscious bondage hindering my spiritual and physical growth.

2 I take authority against the following:
   a. Self-deception
   b. Depression
   c. Oppression
   d. Pride
   e. Fear
   f. Doubt
   g. Confusion
   h. Rejection
   i. Untimely death
   j. Hopelessness
   k. Immorality

3 Enough to the following Generational:
   a. Poverty
   b. Set back
   c. Late marriage
   d. Sickness
   e. Disease
   f. Tears
   g. Sorrows

h. Pains
   i. Frustration
   j. Carry over

4 God make me a pillar in my family.

5 Thank God for answering prayers.

Show Yourself Oh God

Scriptural Reading: 1 Kings 18 1 - end

Prayer Points

1. Sing praises to God for his miracle that is beyond human understanding, worship Him from the whole of your heart and be grateful to Him.

2. I charge all the doors through which he enemy has been passing to inflict pains and sorrow in my life to be closed permanently.

3. Evil priest of Baal throwing stones into my affair, God prove yourself by sending your fire of vengeance in Jesus mighty name.

4. Every Pharaoh of this generation who does not allow me to cross over to my Canaan land God let your red sea consume them in Jesus mighty name.

5. Every greatness in me that has been caged, Jehovah show yourself that the world may know that you are God.

6. Every king Josiah that wants to stop my glory from shinning, God prove yourself in Jesus mighty name.

Removing Evil Marks

Scriptural Reading: Mark 10:46 - end

Prayer Points

1. Give quality thanks and songs of praise to God for His power to set the captive free.

2. Take some minutes to meditate on the power that is in the blood of Jesus.

3. Now begin to plead the blood of Jesus over your life, family, and everything that concerns you.

4. I command every demonic mark on my forehead to be removed now in Jesus mighty name.

5. Evil mark from demonic kingdom causing sorrow and pains in my life (mention the following in prayer).
    a. Pains
    b. Sorrow
    c. Late marriage
    d. Childlessness
    e. Sickness
    f. Poverty
    g. Set-back
    h. Stagnation
    i. Tears
       Promise and fail

Promise and Fail

A lot of individuals are facing promise and fail. In other words, all the promises they have received none has been manifested. When this problem called "Promise and Fail" keep reoccurring then you should know that something is wrong somewhere. Thus the following prayer points will ensure your freedom from this cankerworm called Promise and Fail.

Prayer Points

1   Every arrow of promise and fail targeting my destiny, catch fire in Jesus mighty name.

2   God change my name today from promise to fulfillment in Jesus mighty name.

3   Every Satanic agent strategically positioned to break my heart through unkept promises, you will never see me in Jesus mighty name.

4   God open my eyes to see and know these agents of unkept promises.

5   Every cause of unkept promises in my life, your chapter is closed in Jesus mighty name.

Divine Healing

Scriptural Reading: Isaiah 53:5

It is God's will to heal his people. Jesus said that healing is the children's bread. It is important to have faith in God's word that God is able to do what he promised he will do. As you take these prayers I see you being healed in Jesus name. The blood of Jesus that speaks better things than that of Abel will speak healing to your life today. Remember to him that believes, all things are possible.

Prayer Points

1. According to your word, I release healing to my body, spirit, and soul.

2. I drink the blood of Jesus by faith and I decree:
   a. Every deposit of Satan in my belly
   b. Every evil load on my head thereby causing headache catch fire in Jesus name

3. Healing is the children's bread, Father I ask for my portion in Jesus mighty name.

4. Whatever that has made my marriage to go sick, God I ask that you heal it in Jesus name.

5   May the stripes of Jesus bring healing today in my life.

6   I declare that I am healed in the morning, day and night.

Academic Success

Scriptural Reading: Psalms 119:99

Daniel 1:17 - 20

Prayer Points

1. Praise and worship God for his goodness and mercy endure forever.

2. Remember that wisdom comes from God thus, ask him to baptize you with wisdom and understanding towards your academic success.

3. I receive wisdom today in Jesus mighty name.

4. From today I will have answers to questions in my examinations.

5. The God who gave wisdom to Daniel visit me in Jesus mighty name.

6. No more carry-over in works.

7. Anointing for excellence be released on me in Jesus mighty name.

8. I bind the spirit of fear and confession beginning from this hour.

9. Almighty perfect my studies in Jesus name.

10. I command the giant in me to wake-up.

11 God sharp-up my memory in Jesus mighty name.

12 Let the spirit of diligent visit me in the course of my lectures.

Shake Them Away

Scriptural Reading: Haggai 2:6 – 7

Prayer Points

1. Thank God for His power and His greatness to set the captive free.

2. Pray against the following:
   a. The poison of any king whether hidden or open
   b. Spiritual load in any department of my life
   c. Evil council summoned against me.
   d. Spiritual husband/wife
   e. Powers of marriage destruction

3. God fill me with the power and let self-disappear for you to appear.

4. God shake away every stubborn pursuer away from my life.

5. I command al spiritual remote control against to be shaken away no in Jesus name.

6. Every garment of shame on my body, I shake you away in Jesus name wonderful name.

7. Holy Spirit take away every wrong foundation attacking my destiny in Jesus name.

8   I withdraw all my properties from the hand of Satan in Jesus name.

9   Every Satanic deposit in my blood, I shake you away now in Jesus name

10 Every problem attached to my name, shake away now in Jesus mighty name.

11 Thank God for answering all the prayers.

Deliverance from Temptation

Prayer Points

1. In everything, give thanks to God who is able, the godly from all temptation according to His word.

2. Father deliver me from all temptations.

3. Give me the grace to jump any temptation that may come my way.

4. God deliver me from the sins of:
    a. Fornication
    b. Adultery
    c. Stealing
    d. Masturbation
    e. Lying
    f. Idolatry
    g. Drunkenness
    h. Fighting

5. Lord grant me the grace to avoid quarrel and fighting.

6. I reject the spirit of:
    a. Gossip
    b. The pride that leads to a fall
    c. Self-exaltation

7. I pray for the spirit of meekness to take over my life.

8   Every pit strategically prepared by the enemy to swallow me, be scattered in Jesus mighty name.

9   I receive power to rise above every stumbling block kept for me by the agent of Satan.

10 My mouth will never take me to the prison in Jesus name.

11

    My legs will never step on any temptation in Jesus name.

Pursue and Recover

Scriptural Reading: 1 SAMUEL 30:1 - end

Prayer Points

1. Give thanks to God for His love and kindness towards you.

2. Sing songs of praise to Him. Remember the Lord inhabits the praise of His people.

3. Father, I overtake all my over takers in Jesus name.

4. Holy Spirit release speed on my legs in order to run faster than all my pursuers.

5. I recover all my lost glory in Jesus name.

6. God, arm me with the spirit of courage to go on in spite of all the discouragement in life in Jesus mighty name.

7. I stop every Goliath that wants to stop me.

8. Every demonic vehicle loading away my blessing, catch fire and break down now in Jesus mighty name.

9. Every Satanic robber of my destiny be disgraced in Jesus name.

10 Let blessing, mercy, love, goodness and financial prosperity from God pursue and overtake me now in Jesus mighty name.

11 Begin to thank God for answering prayers.

Prayer

Let there be a divine intervention in all that concerns you. May you be moved into the circles that will enhance your status and improve your life spiritually, financially, educationally, maritally and in your ministry. I impart the peace of the Lord on your life. Let the light of the Word of God shine and break up all influences of negative circles in your life.

Contact Gloria and Larry Ovie

We love you and are waiting to hear from you.

Please, get in touch with us:

Tel: + 353 (0)8 9959 8112

Email: larry_2000a1@yahoo.com

Web: http://www.larryovieministry.com

Other Books by Larry Ovie

The Power of a Circle

It's Too Late to Fail

Is Blessing Now a Cost?

Available worldwide from all good bookstores

---

http://mtp.agency

http://facebook.com/mtp.agency

@mtp_agency

www.ingramcontent.com/pod-product-compliance
Lightning Source LLC
LaVergne TN
LVHW040151080526
838202LV00042B/3116